Dartmoor's History

Paul White

Bossiney Books

This reprint 2019

First published 2018 by
Bossiney Books Ltd, 67 West Busk Lane, Otley, LS21 3LY
www.bossineybooks.com

Part of this book is based on the author's *Medieval Dartmoor*

ISBN 978-1-906474-68-3

Acknowledgements
Artwork is by Graham Hallowell.
The photograph on page 3 is by Robert Hesketh.
All other photographs are by the author.

Printed in Great Britain by R Booth Ltd, Penryn, Cornwall

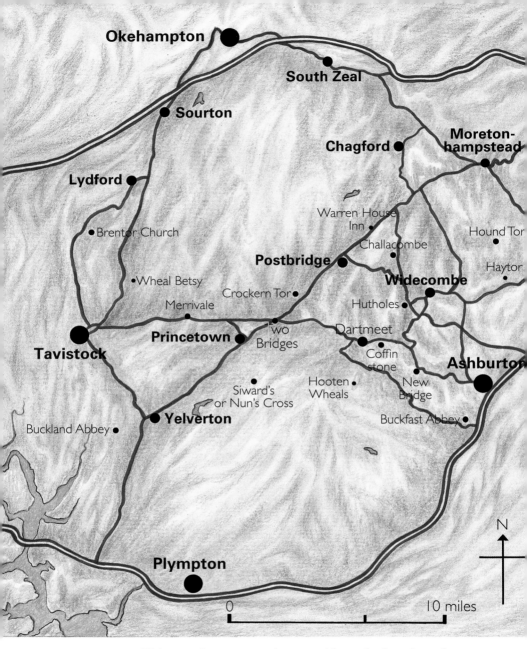

Okehampton

South Zeal

Sourton

Moreton-
hampstead

Chagford

Lydford

Warren House
Inn

Hound Tor

Brentor Church

Challacombe

Haytor

Postbridge

Wheal Betsy

Widecombe

Crockern Tor

Hutholes

Merrivale

Princetown

Two
Bridges

Dartmeet

Coffin
stone

Tavistock

Ashburton

Hooten
Wheals

New
Bridge

Siward's
or Nun's Cross

Yelverton

Buckfast Abbey

Buckland Abbey

N

Plympton

0   10 miles

*This map is an approximate guide to the location of
places mentioned in the text*

2

Challacombe near Grimspound. In certain lights, especially in winter, the remains of a medieval field system can be clearly seen. A small settlement now stands where once there was a whole village.

Introduction

Dartmoor has been exploited by people for some 6000 years. For much of that time the higher ground was mostly used for summer grazing, but there have been a few periods when areas of it were settled and cultivated – notably the Bronze Age and the Middle Ages, especially from about AD 900-1350. Climate change and population pressures were the decisive factors.

Attempts were made in the century after 1780 to populate the moorland again and to develop both agriculture and industry.

Mineral extraction has been practised over a much wider time span, but has been of highly variable significance.

The prehistoric period is covered in my book *Ancient Dartmoor*. The present book touches briefly on the 'Dark Ages' but deals mostly with the medieval and modern periods. It suggests a number of places on Dartmoor which you will hopefully find worth a visit, illustrating various aspects of moorland life such as farming and industry, communications and housing.

Ordnance Survey grid references are given: the 1:25,000 Outdoor Leisure Map is definitely worth buying.

Post-Roman and medieval Dartmoor

Dartmoor's upland population was already far smaller in Roman times than it had been 1500 years earlier. Then in the sixth century a series of plagues swept through Europe, and seem to have afflicted south-western Britain and Wales particularly badly.

One intriguing possibility is that dust clouds from a massive eruption of Krakatoa around AD 540 created a 'volcanic winter', bringing famine, weakness and disease as its inevitable consequence. But what is fairly certain is that at about this time substantial numbers emigrated from Devon and Cornwall to Brittany, which was underpopulated and had suffered less from the plague. It seems likely that the whole of Devon was very thinly populated for several centuries afterwards.

Into this near-deserted landscape came 'Saxon' settlers from Wessex, who easily found good quality land which had been abandoned. It is possible that the settlement of Devon was mainly peaceful, although later on there were battles either side of the river Tamar. With much better farmland readily available, there was no immediate need to re-colonise Dartmoor.

We have insufficient evidence either archaeological or historical to know exactly how and when the Saxons settled around or on the moor. The old idea that fair-haired German warriors with their families invaded Britain and forced 'the Celts' into the western and northern hills is now doubted by most historians. There may even have been as few as 50,000 'Saxon' immigrants in the whole of England, but they were disproportionately powerful.

Early Wessex probably contained very few of these newcomers. Its people had once spoken 'British' (which became Welsh/Cornish/Breton) and a bit of Latin if they were gentry or merchants. Now they adopted the economically dominant language which replaced Latin – 'Anglo-Saxon'.

Dumnonia (the British kingdom of Devon and Cornwall) lost control of Devon to Wessex somewhere between AD 650 and 700.

At this time it is likely that the whole Dartmoor area was almost uninhabited, with just a few farming families (probably British-speaking) eking out a living on its borders.

The only substantial settlement we know of was at Lydford, where the church is dedicated to St Petrock, a 'Celtic' saint, which suggests an early origin. Quite possibly (though there is a lack of evidence) Lydford was benefitting from the tin industry. By 900 it had become a Saxon *burh* (defended town), one of only four in Devon. In 977 it withstood a Viking raiding force which sacked Tavistock Abbey.

By the time of Domesday Book in 1086 the centre of the moor (the royal 'Forest') was still uninhabited, but farms such as Natsworthy (SX721800) were being ploughed at 370 metres altitude. The late Saxon period saw a great extension of agriculture into areas which had been abandoned for the previous 2000 years, and this trend continued after 1066.

The expansion was propelled by population growth and for a time assisted by an improving climate.

But by 1300 the climate was again worsening. Medieval farmers needed to be self-sufficient. As well as tending animals, they had to grow corn and vegetables. This became harder as rainfall levels increased. When the Black Death struck in 1348-9 and a third of the population died, land at lower altitudes became available which could be cultivated with less risk of crop failures. The oppressive system which tied workers to the land began to crumble, allowing many to escape.

Many hamlets and farmsteads – if they had not already been abandoned before 1348 – were deserted at this time, but by no means all. Some were deserted in later centuries, but many still exist today. Occasionally the original buildings survive, perhaps as farm outbuildings.

Longhouses

The characteristic medieval Dartmoor building is the longhouse. Remains of the earliest examples can be seen at two excavated and beautifully presented medieval hamlets, Hound Tor (SX746788) and Hutholes (SX702759). At these abandoned sites it is possible to get some idea of how life must have been around 1300.

Longhouses were built on a slope, and combined living quarters for people (locally known as the 'livier') at the upper end, and for

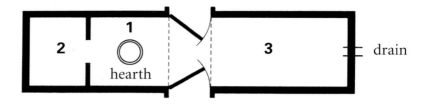

1: living room or 'livier' **2:** working area **3:** shippon

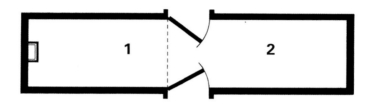

Simplified plans of a longhouse (top) and cross-passage house (below)

animals (the 'shippon') at the lower end, with a sluice drain in the lower end wall. The longhouse was single storey. Its livier was often just one room, as was the shippon, and the division between them was not necessarily a wall of full height. It is reckoned that a cow puts out as much heat as a single-bar electric fire and this heat was very welcome. Given no windows and a peat fire smoking on the central hearth, it must have been truly cosy.

The entrance or entrances served man and beast alike. In later examples, an inner room is found – not, as you might imagine, a bedroom, but of more practical use as a storeroom or dairy – and 'outshot' or lean-to rooms might be added still later.

The other common type of medieval farmhouse is the 'cross passage house' in which there is a living room at either end, and a cross passage between a front door and a back door – with the animals in a separate building outside. It was possible for a house to be converted from one style to the other. Animals might be expelled to a separate building as a family grew richer.

At Hound Tor the largest longhouse, often referred to as the 'manor house', is the one furthest from the Hound Tor rocks, 17.5 metres long by just 4 metres wide and divided into three rooms.

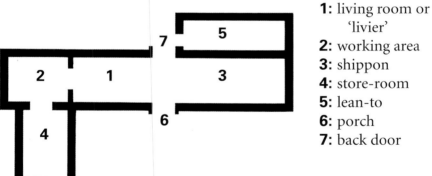

1: living room or 'livier'
2: working area
3: shippon
4: store-room
5: lean-to
6: porch
7: back door

The livier has an inner room and the shippon has a central drain. But this building was originally constructed as a two room cross-passage house, and was subsequently converted to accommodate the cattle in the former living room. Perhaps the family fortunes had declined. Or maybe the 'squire' had moved downhill to a more sheltered location, leaving his old house to junior members of the family?

The four Hound Tor longhouses and their outbuildings were built in the 13th century: they replaced earlier buildings, probably of turf which was used when wood was unavailable. The manor was owned by Tavistock Abbey and included at least one other small settlement with a longhouse and barns (SX 745791).

Domesday Book tells us that in 1086 Hound Tor's tenant under the Abbot was Rainald, who also held many other manors: at Hound Tor he had two slaves and two 'villeins' (villagers) working for him, and there were also four 'bordars' (smallholders). Women and children were not enumerated. None of them were free to leave this land. There were also 2 ploughs, 7 cattle, 28 sheep and 12 goats.

Longhouses are not unique to Dartmoor, but here they survive in larger numbers than elsewhere – more than a hundred are known. This is probably because they were built of enduring granite at a time of relative prosperity, then survived centuries of poverty and so were neither replaced nor converted beyond recognition. Sometimes the whole of the old longhouse was used for farm purposes while a new range or a cross-wing was added at the upper end.

A longhouse at Hutholes, with cooking hearth at far end on the left

A particularly fine surviving longhouse: Jordan (SS700750)

Farming

It is just possible to see the typical vestiges of medieval ploughing at Hound Tor – parallel ridge and furrow marks. These identify strips of land which 'belonged' to different families. The ploughman circled round the strip, and the mould-board of the plough threw the soil up to one side, forming a ridge in the middle and furrows either side. The furrows helped drain the land. It was a survival strategy: in a drought a crop might survive in the damp furrow, in a wet year the plants on the ridge would do best.

The fields would have been worked communally, whatever the exact details of 'ownership' of the crops on each strip. These people must have been totally dependent on each other, and the more agreeable lifestyle of Rainald and the abbots of Tavistock depended on them.

Part of their work was to wrest additional arable land from the 'waste', or hitherto unfarmed land. Although they needed to grow their own crops, their main business would have been their sheep, goats and cattle which grazed on the unenclosed moor in summer.

Medieval maps of Dartmoor showed the moor schematically as

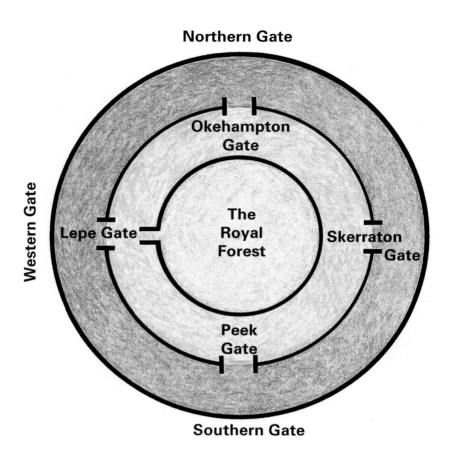

Northern Gate

Okehampton Gate

Western Gate

Lepe Gate

The Royal Forest

Skerraton Gate

Peek Gate

Southern Gate

concentric circles: the diagram above is based on a map of about 1550 which has been re-drawn and the text edited for clarity (taking some liberties in the process: the original appears in *Early Devon Maps* by Mary Ravenhill and Margery Rowe).

Another agricultural activity which has left relics on Dartmoor is the rabbit warren. These were quite numerous, always owned by a land-owner or a religious house, and usually looked after by a warrener, one of whose duties must have been to prevent poaching.

The warren consisted of a number of 'pillow mounds' in which earth was piled up in sufficient quantity for a colony of rabbits to feel safe inside. Burrowing in this loose, well drained earth must have been rather easier than on the natural moor. Cleverly designed traps were built to ensnare vermin.

A 'pillow mound', part of a rabbit warren

The schematic structure of a parish. The population lives at or near the lowest point. Above the village are its open fields, as well as enclosed land belonging to individuals. Above that is an area of pasture to which only the villagers have grazing rights. Above that again, beyond the parish boundary, is 'The Forest' in which almost everyone in Devon had grazing rights

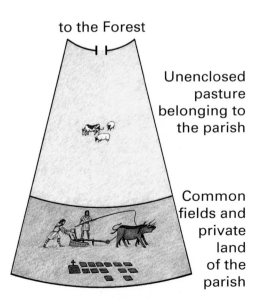

to the Forest

Unenclosed
pasture
belonging to
the parish

Common
fields and
private
land
of the
parish

Communications

At a very early period – probably in the Bronze Age – drove roads were established which allowed outsiders access to the high moor without disturbing the village communities on its fringes. Every farmer in Devon seems to have had grazing rights on Dartmoor – except the burghers of Barnstaple and Totnes. Still more tracks led from each village onto its own part of the moor.

Many of these tracks still survive in one form or another. One of the most evocative I have walked is that which leads from near South Brent (you can pick it up at SX 684603) to Corringdon Ball Gate.

Medieval Dartmoor was no 'trackless waste'. It was criss-crossed with paths and tracks suitable for people on foot or horseback, for trains of pack animals, or for loads pulled on sledges. Wheeled vehicles were not used in most parishes until the nineteenth century.

Some of the long-distance tracks can still be traced today: the photograph below shows part of a track over Yartor Down, above Dartmeet (park at SX 680733 and walk due west) showing the typical hollow created by centuries of use.

A straight medieval holloway beside the bendy modern road

Crosses often mark the line of a track: this is Siward's or Nun's Cross

Half way up the hill east from Dartmeet (SX 677733) stands the Coffin Stone. When someone died in this part of the Forest, their corpse had to be carried to Widecombe Church along the Lich Path. (Before 1260 it had to be carried all the way to Lydford, which in winter was 25 km (15 miles), even further than to Widecombe!)

It was traditional even into the twentieth century to rest the coffin on the Coffin Stone. Legend tells that the stone was cloven in two by a lightning bolt when a particularly sinful corpse was resting there.

Our ancestors generally chose the straight route to walk up or down a hill: the zig-zag approach, reducing the gradient, only came in when roads were reconstructed for wheeled traffic, often in the late eighteenth or early nineteenth century, and at many places in Devon you can spot the old track plunging headlong downhill as a bridle-way while the tarmac road snakes back and forth across it.

The river crossing might be a ford or a 'clapper bridge', a primitive structure heavy enough to resist the river when it is in flood. Most of the clapper bridges seen today are unlikely to be original, but are probably replacements for earlier and similar structures. Even modern bridges can be destroyed by violent floods, so it is amazing any have survived at all. Dartmoor's finest clapper bridge is at Postbridge: see cover photograph.

New Bridge

Everything must have been new at some time. New Bridge, like nearby Holne Bridge, was 'new' around 1415. Building bridges of this quality was clearly a major expense and presumably done at a time of great prosperity in the tin and/or cloth industries.

Medieval bridges were often constructed by wealthy people at the suggestion of priests or monks: it was very good for the soul – an assured quick route to heaven. No better way of funding roads and bridges was found until the mid-eighteenth century, when turnpikes promised investors a direct route to more earthly profits.

Another helpful but rather cheaper way to save your soul was by erecting a cross as a waymark, and these are numerous on Dartmoor. They were doubly useful if placed where two tracks crossed, or if they marked a parish or estate boundary as well as the line of a track. Some may have had a previous existence as ancient standing stones and been reshaped to proclaim the new faith.

Other crosses around the moor served a different purpose. They were set up in settlements before a church had been built, perhaps in the sacred enclosure (*lan* in the British language): the church-yard as an enclosure often pre-dates the church. Some crosses were established as village preaching points, and after the church had been built they might become the secular centre of the village.

Abbeys and churches

The Church played an important part in medieval life on the secular level as well as the religious. The three abbeys of Tavistock, Buckfast and Buckland, the very wealthy priory at Plympton and the Bishop of Exeter between them owned vast amounts of land, including many villages on the borders of Dartmoor. Tavistock Abbey's annual income was little short of £1000 at the Dissolution of the monasteries: this compares with the Devon income of the richest south-west landowner at the time, Henry Courtenay, which was £1300.

Tavistock Abbey was founded in the 970s. Its buildings covered a huge area – most of what is today central Tavistock. Only fragments remain, including the gateway now known as 'Betsy Grimbal's Tower' and the wall and Still Tower beside the river. There had been a small settlement at Tavistock before the monks arrived, but it was the abbot who initiated the Friday market and annual fair and, around 1160, had it made into a borough.

Buckland Abbey lies just off the moor today, near Yelverton, but the unenclosed moor extended much further when the abbey was founded in 1278. After the Dissolution some of its buildings, including a wonderful barn, survived as part of Sir Richard Grenville's country house, which was bought by Sir Francis Drake in 1581. It is now a National Trust property.

Buckfast Abbey was founded in 1018 by King Cnut. By 1100 it had ceased to exist but was refounded 1134-6 as a Cistercian house. Its annual income at the Dissolution was £486. Buckfast was refounded as a modern Benedictine Abbey in 1902, and a new church was built. The rejuvenated abbey attracts many visitors.

All the medieval abbeys exploited their vast properties much as contemporary secular owners did – but often with greater skill. They farmed manors, founded borough towns and encouraged the growth of local industries, all with a view to maximising their incomes.

The early abbeys in Devon, as elsewhere, were mainly founded by kings. Abbots were often a member of the royal family who had been 'offered' to the Church as a child. His family expected

The church and church house at Widecombe-in-the-Moor

him to live in a style becoming to his birth and the abbey had to be endowed with great estates to make this possible. It is quite likely that the re-colonisation of Dartmoor in the tenth century stemmed at least in part from grants of under-used royal land to the abbeys, and from the abbots' wish to make the most of their new property.

The spiritual needs of the population outside the monastic walls were the responsibility not of the abbeys, but of the bishop and the parish clergy. The photograph above shows the church and church house at Widecombe-in-the-Moor, a huge parish. From 1260 this church also served the inhabitants of the eastern side of the Forest,

Centuries of tin extraction have left visible damage in many parts of the moor. This is Whiteworks, not far from Princetown

who should theoretically have gone to Lydford church – all 22,700 hectares (56,000 acres) of the Forest were part of Lydford parish until 1987.

Because long walks to church were quite normal, church houses were built to accommodate the parishioners between services, and to provide refreshments. Naturally they became a focus of village life and in many Devon villages they have been preserved as the village inn. That at Widecombe was built in 1537, and now houses a National Trust shop and a room which serves as a village hall.

The tin industry

Tin was certainly being exploited on Dartmoor by AD 1150, and quite possibly earlier; for the next fifty years it was a very important industry, and was worked under special Stannary Laws (Latin *stannum* = tin) which both taxed the trade and at the same time gave the tinners privileges and encouragement.

The subject is a complicated one, and the following account is highly simplified.

In the early days the only method of obtaining the ore was by 'streaming'. By scouring the stream beds, the tinners found black

stones containing tin ore, or they could pan gravel for it, rather like prospectors in the Gold Rush. The tin ore (cassiterite) is far heavier than other rock, so it can be separated by gravity if the gravel is swirled around in water.

The ore was then crushed using horizontal round millstones in a building called a crazing-house: the technique was borrowed from corn-milling. The ore was crudely smelted on site, then transported to a 'stannary town' for further smelting under official supervision. Chagford, Ashburton, Plympton and Tavistock were the stannary towns, each with jurisdiction over a sector of the moor.

For a few years in the 1180s Devon was a major player in the world tin market, but the deposits near the surface were soon used up. Production fell steeply so new methods were gradually introduced to improve the yields.

The tinners sought out the 'lodes' from which the ore in the stream-beds had been broken, and followed them back into the hillside, creating great scars down the hill. They dug test pits in likely areas, many of which proved barren and were left unfilled. Much of today's apparently natural Dartmoor landscape is in reality the half-healed scars of the tin industry.

Once the ore began to be brought out as rock rather than gravel, machinery was invented to break it up. Opposite you can see the method in use from about 1300-1580, the 'dry stamps'. An overshot waterwheel powers a row of metal-shod poles which rise and fall onto a stone base, crushing the ore. Smelting was now turned into a single process, carried out on the moor in a 'blowing house'. The 'blowing' refers to bellows, powered by a water wheel, which raised the temperature in a furnace fuelled by charcoal, made from peat.

Some of the best examples of blowing houses are those at Merrivale. The first 'Lower Merrivale blowing house' is at SX 553754 and its ruins are shown in the photograph below.

Tin ore was delivered to the uphill end of the building (on the right of the photo). The two upright slabs set in the cross-wall are the remains of the furnace. Tipped up at an angle is a 'floatstone' (apparently one of only two to survive) which should be flat, and in which there is a shallow trough. The molten ore dribbled out into that trough and was then ladled into the 'mould stone' (today full of rain-water). The ingot of tin was then allowed to cool in the mould, ready to be transported to a stannary town for taxation.

At the next blowing house, SX 553762, you will find much the same arrangement but with a clearly defined water-wheel pit. There is a further pair of buildings – a 'knocking mill' with stamps and a blowing house – at SX 552766 if you are feeling energetic.

All three Merrivale sites were probably active in the early Tudor period, when there was a minor boom in Dartmoor tin production peaking in 1524, though they may have continued into the 17th century. Very sensibly production ceased in the winter months!

The importance of water in powering this industry can hardly be exaggerated. Each waterwheel required a leat (artificial water-course) to deliver a constant flow of water. Everywhere you walk on Dartmoor you will find leats, some ancient and dry, some still flowing, winding along the contours to a mystery destination.

The tinners were so favoured by successive monarchs that they were no longer answerable, in most things, to the same law-code as other people. They had their own Parliament, their own laws and their own courts. Woe betide a non-tinner who got caught up in the 'justice' of the stannary courts at Lydford.

The tinners' independence was such that when Richard Strode, Plympton's MP in the 1512 Westminster Parliament, tried to stop mining near the seaports because the waste it created was choking the harbours, he found himself locked up in the notorious stannary prison of Lydford Castle (which you can still visit – no fee).

There was an ancient rhyme which ran:

> I oft have heard of Lydford law
> Where in the morn they hang and draw
> And sit in judgement after.

It probably referred to much earlier courts which applied the harsh

A leat in Tavy Cleave

Forest Law, but the stannary courts did their best to follow the same principles.

Now for one of the most bizarre features of medieval Dartmoor – Crockern Tor (SX616758). This not very distinctive tor is near the road and makes an easy climb with pleasant views, but it was once the venue at which the stannary parliaments met.

The stannary boundaries converged just a little further south but the tor is roughly equidistant from each of the stannary towns, and was accessible by the packhorse routes. The earliest meeting recorded here was in 1494. Nearly a hundred representatives used to meet on the summit, with the Vice-Warden of the Stannaries in the chair (metaphorically).

It is likely that most men who actually got their hands dirty in the tin industry were part-timers, combining streaming with farm-work. The representatives at the stannary parliaments, on the other hand, were usually landowners or merchants from the towns.

Of the four stannaries, Chagford was the most important until the 1460s, when Ashburton took over. In the post-medieval period, Tavistock grew increasingly important.

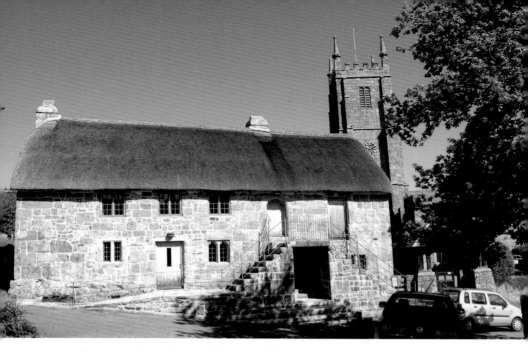

The church and church house of South Tawton, within which parish the 'town' of South Zeal was created

The growth of towns

Most towns started as speculative ventures. Landowners hoped they could make more profit by letting out land in towns to 'burghers', and holding a weekly market and an annual fair, than by letting or farming the land on which the town stood.

The embryo town was laid out methodically in 'burgage plots', usually long thin strips running back from a road. The road frontage, where the burgher could set up a shop front, was what made the land valuable.

If the new town was a success, further roads were built and the long plots might be sub-divided, with new roads parallel to the first. Many 'towns' never developed beyond village status and here the initial plan may be visible – as it is in South Zeal which is still part of the parish of South Tawton. South Zeal lies along what was once the main Exeter to Okehampton road.

The 1:25,000 OS map shows clearly its remarkable layout. If you climb up Cosdon Beacon (and it is quite a climb, to 550 m, 1800 ft) you can see how South Zeal's gardens are still long and thin. On a particularly fine day you can, I believe, see from Cosdon both the English Channel and the Bristol Channel, as well as the beautiful Bronze Age triple stone row at SX 643916 if you still need tempting!

At Tavistock and Ashburton woollen cloth was manufactured from the local Dartmoor wool, and both towns benefited from the twice yearly 'coinages' of tin, as did Chagford. Lydford was more important than it now is, being the administrative centre for the royal Forest. Okehampton was tiny, dependent on its baronial castle. Moretonhampstead and Bovey Tracey, though technically 'boroughs', probably did not develop into real towns until the late 16th century.

Not one of these 'towns' had a total population over 500 and apart from their churches they now have little to see of medieval date, but much from later, more dynamic stages of their history. Chagford, though, has a 'medieval feel' and some early Tudor buildings.

Lydford Castle, once the administrative centre of the moor

The post-medieval period, 1500-1790

The agricultural population declined sharply after the Black Death. Although mining continued, many of those in the industry would have walked to work from the surrounding villages, perhaps camping out at the mines in the summer months, and by the mid-seventeenth century output had in any case become negligible. Quarrying for granite, as opposed to using surface stone, had not yet started.

The population on the moor in this period was consequently tiny and dispersed. Dartmoor seems to have acquired a reputation as an isolated and dangerous place, with the Brent Tor area in particular supposedly inhabited by a terrifying predatory gang of people called Gubbins, whose 'language is the dross of the dregs of the vulgar Devonian' and 'whose wealth consisteth of other men's goods'.

Gubbins remains a local surname. No evidence has ever emerged to explain the origin of the story in the 1660s. Dr Richard Pococke, having visited Devon in 1750, wrote that 'The people about this moor are as civilised as in other parts (tho' vulgarly reputed otherwise).'

If the Gubbins myth was not enough to deter visitors to the moor, the state of the 'roads' surely would have been. There was a post-road from Exeter via Postbridge to Tavistock, but in 1675 the great authority on post-roads, John Ogilby, said

> The way is indifferent good to Chegford [sic] tho' hilly, but after over Dart-Moor to Tavistoke exceeding bad, being hilly, boggy and stony: thence to Truro 'tis indifferent good again and is everywhere (except on Dartmoor) furnished with good Inns.

By contrast, he thought the route via Chudleigh, Ashburton and South Brent was 'in general a very good road'. Considering the negative comments that South Brent road received from contemporary travellers such as Celia Fiennes, the Dartmoor road must have been bad indeed.

So most people avoided the Tavistock-Moretonhampstead road.

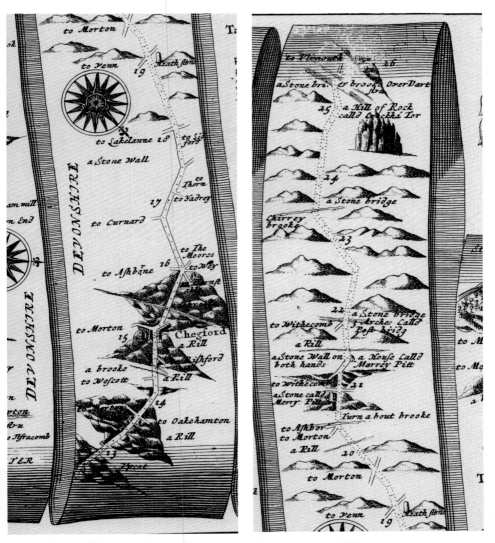

John Ogilby's road map for crossing Dartmoor in 1675

Efforts to improve it began in 1771, but the work was not completed until 1798, and the Plymouth road from Roborough to Two Bridges was not turnpiked till 1812. As late as 1867, Samuel Smiles wrote:

> The difficulties of road-engineering in that quarter, as well as the sterility of a large proportion of the moor, had the effect of preventing its becoming opened up to modern

traffic; and it is accordingly curious to find how much of its old manners, customs, traditions and language has been preserved. It looks like a piece of England of the Middle-Ages, left behind on the march... The upland road or track [from Chagford] to Tavistock scales an almost precipitous hill, and though well adapted for the pack-horse of the last century, it is quite unfitted for the cart and waggon traffic of this. Hence the horse with panniers maintains its ground in the Chagford district; and the double-horse, furnished with a pillion for the lady riding behind, is still to be met with in the country roads.

The age of improvement

In the absence of serious interest in the moor in the 17th and 18th centuries, it is unsurprising that the holders of the 'ancient tenements', who had the historic right to enclose 8 acres of common land every time a new generation inherited, began by some means to enclose much larger areas, as much as 75 acres at a time. The 'tenants' were people like Sir Thomas Leare and Sir Gervase Lucas, who certainly were not the actual workers on the farms. Country estates were in the making.

The losers when common land was enclosed were the ordinary commoners. From the seventeenth century the Duchy was happy to allow such developments, which helped its finances. In the 18th century enclosure became a national phenomenon, greatly to the benefit of the larger landowners, but now justified on the grounds of 'improvement'.

It was certainly true that a landowner had an incentive to 'improve' land which he individually controlled, an incentive which did not exist where land was held in common, and the result was far greater yields of both crops and livestock. This was good for a nation with an increasing population, as well as for the landowner's pocket. But not for the poor, who lost their grazing rights in the process.

Whilst Dartmoor was comparatively late to be developed, once the process had begun the moorland proprietors showed themselves very enthusiatic for experiment.

The century of exploitation, 1790-1900

Although he was not alone, one man stands out in the transformation of Dartmoor – Sir Thomas Tyrwhitt (1762-1833). At university he became a friend of the Prince of Wales, later to become Prince Regent and later still George IV, and Tyrwhitt was granted 2500 acres at Tor Royal. As well as being private secretary to the Prince (and sorting out the Prince's financial woes when he separated from his wife) he was secretary and auditor of the Duchy, Lord Warden of the stannaries, and MP for Okehampton, as well as holding many sinecures.

Judge Francis Buller, who held nearby Prince's Hall, and the Gullett family who ran the Prince's Hall farm, had already been making agricultural experiments which were highly thought of, though by no means always successful.

Tyrwhitt hoped to demonstrate that Dartmoor could be fertile, and could become a well-populated area, to the advantage both of himself and the Duchy, whose annual income from Dartmoor was a pathetic £43. Whilst one can view him and other landowners cynically, as a man hoping to line his own pocket, there may also have been an altruistic or patriotic aspect. Especially in this time of war, there was a very real need for the nation to become more self-sufficient in its food supply.

There was much scepticism. In 1796 John Laskey, an attorney from Crediton, observed in *The Gentleman's Magazine* that, besides the adverse weather conditions:

> The article of manure will be another great disadvantage
> the incloser and cultivator will labour under; this must
> be deficient in every degree, unless a discovery (almost
> miraculous) should be made of some at present unknown;
> sea-sand and lime are too remote, and dung is impossible
> to be attained in sufficient quantity; neither is gypsum or
> marle to be found in the whole Forest, nor a lime-rock to
> be seen, the whole being a mass of granite or moor-stone.
> Dung, therefore, is the only probable manure that can be
> obtained, and even this not till a considerable degree of

Dartmoor prison, seen across Sir Thomas's enclosures

cultivation has taken place; for should towns arise (by the magical touch of Harlequinism) in the moor, it is presumed their effects, in regard to this manure, would extend but a little way around them.

In time, Francis Buller, Sir Thomas and others demonstrated that Dartmoor *could* be made more fertile – doubtless the war prison produced a useful quantity of dung – but their efforts also showed that it was impossible to make such improvement cost-effective.

Dartmoor reverted to rough grazing – but new and hardier breeds of cattle and sheep were successfully introduced.

One innovation that failed for Francis Buller was forestry, where most of the 40,000 conifers he planted failed to grow. After the First World War, however, the Forestry Commission had more success, planting about 10% of the moor. The plantations still exist. On very hot days, a walk in the conifer woods can be enjoyable, but for many of us these plantations remain something of an eyesore.

Dartmoor Prison

Sir Thomas Tyrwhitt was never averse to an opportunity. When in 1805 it became obvious there was a problem accommodating prisoners-of-war, he proposed building a prison at the new settlement he was planning, Prince's Town (later called Princetown).

Constructing accommodation for 10,000 prisoners, their guards and the numerous other workers who would be needed was never going to be easy, especially when there wasn't a decent road from Plymouth; and Dartmoor's weather in winter, before global warming set in, was even worse than it is today. The inefficiency and stinginess of the navy's Transport Board, which organised the construction, added to the problems.

But by 1809 prisoners were being accepted. Conditions both for prisoners and the building workers were appalling, and 500 prisoners died in a single measles epidemic: finally things got so bad that the Board in the goodness of its heart allowed 2 ounces of soap per prisoner per week (though only for the sick).

Because so little was officially provided, the prisoners had to purchase supplies from the Princetown traders, so for a time the new settlement was successful – but when the wars with France and America ended, the prison suddenly emptied, and almost all the town's inhabitants had to leave. The prison wasn't turned into a convict establishment until 1850.

Transport

Tyrwhitt's next project was the horsedrawn Plymouth & Dartmoor Railway. His prospectus to the Plymouth Chamber of Commerce

The trackbed of the former Princetown Railway

The Haytor tramway

explained its purpose:

> To reclaim, and clothe with grain and grasses a spacious tract of land now lying barren, desolate and neglected; to fill this unoccupied region with an industrious and hardy population; … to provide employment for the poor of several parishes… [These aims] form altogether such a stimulus to [entrepreneurial activity] and such a scope for exertion, especially to a wealthy company, as must dilate the benevolent heart of the patriot, whilst it emboldens the capitalist gladly to lend his assistance in carrying the plan into execution.

Presumably this rhetoric struck a nerve, as the line was opened in 1823, solely for freight. From the beginning, it was the quarries which were the main users. Agricultural improvement on the moor had already largely failed. The line was converted in 1883 to a steam-drawn passenger line, and continued in use until 1956. As with several other former lines on Dartmoor, it now forms an attractive, dry, and relatively flat route for walkers.

On the eastern side of the moor, the Haytor tramway had opened in 1820, specifically to connect the granite quarries there with the Stover Canal. It has a most unusual feature, in that the track itself is made of the hard-wearing local granite rather than of iron.

As the Railway Age began, Dartmoor was gradually surrounded with railways, beginning with Brunel's Totnes to Plymouth line in 1848. Branch lines reached northwards to Moretonhampstead in 1866, and Ashburton in 1872.

To the north of the moor, a line from Exeter reached Okehampton in 1871 and Lydford in 1874, connecting them with Plymouth by 1876 and encircling the moor. Dartmoor, or at least its outer villages, was no longer inaccessible. A new age of tourism would follow.

Mining

New methods of mining, and the demands of an increasingly industrialised Britain for metals, led to renewed activity both on the moor and around its edges, though never on the scale of the industry in Cornwall. Production (of copper, lead and silver, as well as tin) was very dependent on international prices, and tin mining suffered greatly after 1870, though some mines were worked again from 1900 to 1920.

Among the most interesting places to explore the mining activity are near the Warren House Inn (SX682810) and at Hooten Wheals (SX660712) – photo below.

The Wheal Betsy engine house

There is a well maintained Cornish-style engine house at the old copper mine of Wheal Betsy (SX 510812) but this was untypical. It was even more costly to import coal to Dartmoor than to Cornwall, so the Dartmoor mines were mostly worked by waterwheels. Even Wheal Betsy was normally worked by water; the steam engine was there as a back-up in times of drought.

Mining on the southern edge of Dartmoor has not yet stopped. The Drakelands (Hemerdon) mine reopened in 2015, extracting tungsten and tin.

Quarries and peatworks

People had used the surface boulders of Dartmoor granite for four thousand years, but actual quarrying only began in the early nineteenth century, when granite was in demand for prestigious city buildings. When George Templer of Stover, who ran the Haytor quarry (SX755755), won a contract to supply the stone for the new London Bridge, he built the Haytor tramway to transport the stone to the Stover Canal. The quarries at Haytor were in use for the next 40 years.

On the old railway line to Princetown there are three impressive

Merrivale quarry, as seen in 2002 when it had already ceased production. The cranes have since been removed

Foggintor quarry and (below) a china clay works

quarries, Swell Tor (SX 560733), King Tor (SX 554739) and Foggintor (SX 567736), all now thankfully out of use.

On the southern edge of the moor china clay is still extensively quarried, and there also are a number of places, for example Shipley Bridge (SX 681689), where former clay treatment works can be found.

Peat was the traditional fuel of moor dwellers, but in the nineteenth century it was also used for the extraction of naphtha, an

inflammable gas used for lighting. Peatworks were established for this purpose near Princetown (briefly using the prison area as its base) and at Rattlebrook (SX 559872), high above Lydford.

Other industries

Gunpowder, vital to the quarries and mines, was manufactured at the Powder Mills south-west of Postbridge (SX 627774).

Around the edge of the moor there were many more orthodox mills, both for grinding corn and for manufacturing woollen cloth and paper. One fascinating example of water power which survives is Finch Foundry at Sticklepath (SX 642941) which manufactured edge tools, and is now a National Trust property: the machinery is demonstrated regularly throughout the day.

Housing the workers

All these industries required workers. New settlements of industrial housing were built, for example at Foggintor quarry, where a chapel and a school for 50 pupils were provided as well as housing. In some places such as Merrivale and Whiteworks, a few cottages remain, but most are now in ruins and unrecognisable as housing.

This enclosure behind the upper car park at Merrivale has a surprising history – it was once a school!

Reservoirs

Dartmoor's plentiful water supply was tapped by leats to Plymouth in the 16th century and Devonport in the 1790s. In the late 19th and early 20th century reservoirs were created to supply Torquay, Plymouth and Paignton, and there are now eight substantial reservoirs, and many smaller ones, within the National Park.

Tourism and conservation

During the late 18th century, English people had begun to take 'tours' (holidays of exploration) within Britain, partly because of wars abroad, but partly with a genuine wish to understand their own country. Certain areas were favoured, often as being 'picturesque' (which at that time meant 'appropriate for the composition of a painting' – the equivalent of 'photogenic' today) or 'romantic', or 'sublime' which meant inspiring awe. Tourists often went equipped with sketchbooks, pencils and paints.

The most popular areas were the Scottish Highlands, the mountains of north Wales, the Wye valley, and the Lake District. Most of Dartmoor did not fit the criteria, being considered 'dreary', and it was also difficult of access. There was an exception: Lydford Bridge was acknowledged as picturesque, and was compared with Devil's Bridge in Ceredigion.

Gradually, however, improved roads and then the new railways, together with changes in attitudes, brought more visitors and more provision for their requirements. For example, waterfalls were extremely sought after, but visitors in a dry summer were often disappointed. By 1851, the first edition of *Murray's Handbook for Travellers in Devon and Cornwall* says that at 'Lidford Cascade':

> A zigzag walk has been cut to the foot of the cascade; and a miller, who lives hard by, keeps, besides the key of this approach, a certain quantity of water ponded back, which, by the magic of sixpence, may be made to spring over the fall to which it gives an imposing volume and impetuosity.

In 1845, Rachel Evans, daughter of a Presbyterian minister who owned a school in Tavistock, suggested in *Home Scenes: Tavistock and Vicinity* that visitors should base themselves at Princetown where there was 'a good and well-conducted principal inn, besides some decent smaller ones; respectable lodging houses, an omnibus between Exeter and Plymouth, with a ready access to Tavistock'.

> The freshness of unreclaimed nature, the somewhat savage, but yet, in fine weather, cheerful wildness of that wavy expanse of moorland, with its tors for breakers; the absence of all accompaniments of lowland life, produce an effect of novelty, which stimulates the mind as the air does the body, and prompts to movement and activity. Neither is there any lack of objects on which to employ these energies; – the trout stream to the fisherman, the British village, the Druidical Circus, the ancient wood to the antiquarian; the zoology, botany, geology, to the naturalist, are all peculiar, and will tempt each to exercise his several taste. The mere freedom to roam on the greensward, or to climb the rock, will be object enough to the young.

As she suggests, the tourist of this period was interested in many things. Visitors could turn up at a mine and expect to be shown around, and even in some cases go underground.

By the time of the 1872 edition (now at 575 pages nearly twice the length of the first edition) *Murray's Handbook* suggests the

This building in Princetown, now the National Park's Visitor Centre, was formerly the Duchy Hotel. It was here that Conan Doyle stayed in 1901 on his brief visit to the moor

reader should visit the Dartmoor prison (though 'an order, readily procured, from the Home Office is necessary') as well as the local quarries, and mines such as Wheal Friendship.

There is also an increasing interest in the ancient monuments of the moor, and by 1872 they are described in different terms from 1851. At Merrivale, instead of 'a group of Celtic remains, consisting of Druidical circles, processional roads, cromlechs…' Murray's 1871 edition speaks of 'a group of primitive remains consisting of circles, stone avenues, cromlechs…'

From the 1830s onwards, efforts were being made by educated local men to stop the ancient monuments being used as a handy source of granite for fencing or building, and gradually the old antiquarian certainty that the monuments had been used for hideous druid rites such as human sacrifice gave way to an understanding that they were much older, and their purpose was – as it still is – unknown. We can only speculate.

There was at the same time growing pressure for the landscape of the moor to be preserved, rather than exploited by mines, quarries, forestry, the military, and reservoirs to supply the towns. This resulted in 1883 in the foundation of the Dartmoor Preservation Society.

In 1894 London actually attempted to purchase the whole of Dartmoor in order to supply it with fresh water, but this was successfully challenged by the DPA, citing the rights of the commoners.

During the late 19th century and early 20th, awareness of the distinctiveness of Dartmoor was greatly increased, both within Devon and more widely, by the work of William Crossing (1847-1928), Sabine Baring-Gould (1834-1924), the artists William Widgery (1822-1893) and his son Frederick John (1861-1942), and the novelist Eden Phillpotts (1862-1960).

But, for better or worse, the work which has had the most influence over the wider public was written by an author with only a slight acquaintance with the moor – Arthur Conan Doyle's *Hound of the Baskervilles*, published in the *Strand* magazine 1902-3.

In order to create a best-selling gothic novel, Conan Doyle used artistic licence to portray a moor where:

> The longer one stays here the more does the spirit of the moor sink into one's soul, its vastness and also its grim charm. When you are once out upon its bosom you have left all traces of modern England behind you.

Perhaps it is part of Dartmoor's attraction, for people who are not yet familiar with it, that they might encounter fire-breathing hounds, ghostly druids, hairy hands on their steering wheel, or pixies to lead them astray. If so, Conan Doyle certainly did his bit to promote the brand.

The twentieth century

In the early part of the century a few mines survived, but their days were numbered. The china clay industry continued to thrive, however, and greatly damaged the southern edge of the moor.

The 1939-45 war also had a huge impact, with Plymothians taking refuge from the bombing, military camps, prisoner-of-war camps (again), and various defensive measures.

After the war, Dartmoor was designated a National Park, and

*Whilst the conifer plantations were once purely commercial, the
Forestry Commission now tries to make them attractive for visitors*

suddenly everything changed, except in the china clay area, which
was largely excluded from the Park.

There was an attempt to clear up, destroying redundant mine
buildings and abandoned industrial housing, removing rusty
equipment, closing the Princetown railway and ending mineral
mining, though granite quarrying continued at Merrivale into the
1970s and stone dressing continued there until the 1990s.

Is Dartmoor now safe from change? Inevitably there will always
be tensions in any rural area between the exploitation of resources
(which are often the source of local people's livelihoods) and a wish
to preserve the 'natural' landscape.

In the case of Dartmoor, it is not only its National Park status,
but the health and social benefits to the estimated 2.4 million
people who visit each year, and of course the financial benefit to
the local economy resulting from tourism, which tilts the balance
– provided of course that the visitor numbers do not themselves
create new problems.